MIDNIGHT HARVEST
Living in the Moment of Love

by
Frank Hajcak
and

Tricia Garwood

For Dave & Alexis,

May you continue to discover
the depths of love in your relationship

Wishing you many moments
of love. Frank Hajcak

Tricia Garwood

ISBN #978-0-9633616-4-6

Available through: Amazon.com

Special discounts available for fund raising.
Contact:
HumanPotentialPress@yahoo.com

Cover photo by Frank Hajcak

About the Book

Midnight Harvest: Living in the Moment of Love is an illustrated collection of loving dialogues between a husband and wife over a 25 year period. Their entrancing imagery explores the impact of extending the boundaries of romantic emotional love into the metaphysical-spiritual realm, opening the door to love driven by the desire to love more and see each other with the freshness of dawn.

The authors give us a vivid insider's view of two hearts and souls that formed an inseparable bond, living in the moment of love that remains untarnished by events and undiminished by time. Photography and art-work by the authors highlight many of the verses.

Inspired by Elizabeth Barrett and Robert Browning, Frank and Tricia began exchanging simple love notes from which *Midnight Harvest:Living in the Moment of Love* evolved. Choosing romantic places, such as La Sagrada Familia in Barcelona or Machu Picchu in Peru, to exchange poems turned their lives into a series of romantic, loving adventures. The authors stated, "As we explored the geography of the planet we explored the soul of the heart." Midnight Harvest is their map.

Table of Contents

Illustrations

Forethought

Harvesting Love

As we sow, we shall harvest
The seeds we plant in each other's heart
Words that blossom into love
Making us see one another
With the freshness of dawn
Searching for new ways to love.

Reply

In every harvest
Each blossom shall render new seeds
Shaping the course of love
Melding heart to soul
Erasing the barrier between time and eternity.

Midnight Harvest

Prelude

In the awkward silence of our first meeting
A seed fell from your lips
And settled in the recesses of my mind
Where, beyond the light of reason,
Thoughts and images grow from shadows into dreams.

Shadows to Dreams   *Collage by* **Tricia Garwood**

Dream One

Alone- in midnight darkness
I hear your voice calling my name
My heart becomes a fruit laden tree
Bearing gifts for you.
My soul your flute.
Let your breath pass through me
Each note a seed to harvest
In midnight dreams.

Planting Dreams   **Collage by Tricia Garwood**

Dream Two

A golden glow pierces the darkness
Your voice bathed in gentleness fills my heart.
You are spirit, I am flesh
We intertwine as wind and branches
Heart beating on heart singing with a thousand voices
The notes you breathed into my soul.

Dream Three

Softly humming sweet lullabies
You carry my heart gently cupped in your hands
To the wellspring of love.
Your spirit moves through me
Like thread through the eye of a needle
We weave a tapestry of dreams.

Dream Four

I take your face
Gently in my hands and kiss it deeply.
You bid me be your king
With the promise to be my queen,
Vowing: long after everything mortal has faded
Our footprints shall continue
Like a string of pearls across the galaxy.

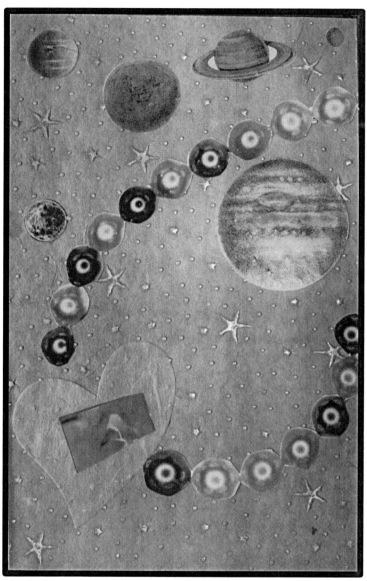

Footprints across the Galaxy   *Collage by* **Tricia Garwood**

Dream Five

Soft angel voices fill the darkness
And with golden thread spin a cocoon
Cradling our hearts and binding our souls
Creating a holy chamber
Echoing notes only soul mates can hear.

Interlude

Floating between dreams
Each chamber of my mind is filled
With phantasmagoric images of you
Creating a tidal wave of love
That breaches the walls of my soul
Making my heart go nova
Seeding the galaxy with stars beyond numbers
That burn for you.

Going Nova   Collage by *Tricia Garwood*

Dream Six

I am a song bird caged in your heart
Sweet notes escape, filling you with thoughts of love
Sending volcanic fire coursing through your veins
We are consumed, reborn like a phoenix
And fly to the amphitheater behind the moon
Where choirs of angels greet soul mates with songs of love.

Dream Seven

My heart
Searching for the pathway to your love
Becomes lost in a labyrinth of dreams within dreams
'till dreamer and dream are one.
The mantra of your voice calling my name
Fills me with hope that I shall
Awaken in your dream.

Labyrinth of Dreams   Collage by **Tricia Garwood**

Dream Eight

As moon shadows evaporate into dawn
I command my heart to take wing
And as a scarlet song bird fly to your chamber
To wake you with sweet notes of love.

Coda

Though my heart is silent now
    In each cell lies a song
        Waiting ....

```
L   T   S   O
I   A   T   F
K   U   R
E   T   I   A
        N
        G   H
        S   A
            R
            P
```

To be released by your hand.
Each note a seed to harvest
In your dreams.

Reply to Dreams

Awake Emperor of my Heart!
I am the light that leads to the wellspring of love,
I will cradle your heart to my breast
And hum sweet lullabies into a tapestry of dreams.
As I play your heartstrings
Heaven's breath will reveal sacred secrets of soul mates.

Reborn of love's fire
Intertwined as wind and branches
Heart beating on heart
We will fly to the amphitheater behind the moon,
And guided by heavenly choirs
Recede into a labyrinth of love
Emerging as soul mates with one dream:
To pursue love's celestial course
As king and queen of the other's heart
Seeding the universe with stars beyond numbers
That burn with love.

Ancient Mystery

You flow through my dreams,
Mysterious night winds
Gently whispering memories preceding time
With the birthing rhythm of ancient tribes.

Reply

Memories of ancient truths
Reflected in your words
Each an amulet casting its spell
Imprinting our hearts with the song of love.

Overload

Thoughts of you arise in my mind
So sweet, so fast
I cannot hold them all.

Faster yet, they come
Like star dust filling the heavens
'Til night outshines the sun.

Reply

Your words
Feed the fire within
Melting the armor that
Protected my heart
Waiting for love.

Riding the Wings of Dawn

Night ends shattering dreams of you.
Creating a void beneath the flame in my heart.

Feeling the ache of aloneness
My heart begs my lips to lie
And say I love you not
And convince my mind
Your face is but a shadow in a receding dream.

Yet the fires of love flow through my veins
Carrying a thousand images of you
I long to hear your voice and know
You are not but a fragment of a midnight dream.

Reply

My heart riding the wings of dawn
Greets you like a songbird with notes of love
Inviting your lips to join my song
Your heart to beat with mine
Your soul to bless this day with love.

Dream Shadows   Photo by **Frank Hajcak**

Genesis

You came into my life
A miracle born of the breath of God
Gifted with love's vision.
Like a queen bestowing her blessing
My name rolled off your lips.
Like courting dolphins breeching the surface in slow motion
We break through time and enter the kingdom of love.

Reply

Gentle as the touch of a feather from an angel's wing
You came into my life – a flower born of starlight
Your fragrance filling me with unearthly joys
I could not fathom.
Your breath whispering visions of love
I could not imagine.
The paths of our pasts mingle like the threads of a tapestry
Woven by love flowing from the heart of heaven.

Reply to Reply

You came, a messenger from a distant star
Cupped hands filled with love's wine
Asking nothing, giving me my fill.
We performed impossible leaps
Pirouetting, waltzing in the cosmic winds
Creating a joyous dance of love with no beginning,
No end.

Life in Vain

Words not spent on you are lost
Darkness dwells where you are not
What good are my eyes but to see you,
My ears but to receive your words
My life but to share with you
But for you heaven would be hell.

Reply

Silently you entered my life
Filling me with so much more than
   The eye can see
   The heart feel
   The mind reason.
As each cell follows its destiny
I come to you overflowing with love.

Whispering Hope

My heart,
  waiting beneath the snow
  for tomorrow's sunrise
  to clear a path to my soul.

Soft as the voice of an angel
Breathing a message of hope
Gently awakening,
My soul
Welcomes your comforting words
Making my heart in its solitude rejoice.

Reply

You are a timeless flower of love
Sent to me through ages
Of torrid summers and frozen winters
Glowing more with each season
Like a sacred apparition about to be revealed.

Timeless Flower   *Photo by **Frank Hajcak***

Connecting

In the middle of a deep dream
Images of you cast from starlight
Standing in the shadow of love's door
One by one finding their home in my heart
Gently cleansing my soul
Like warm spring rains washing away winter snow
Connecting two dreams, two hearts, two souls.

Reply

Words forming in my heart
A poet's song
Love running deep without a sound
Alas! The tongue knows not the language of the heart.

Starlight Images   *Photos by **Frank Hajcak***

The Path to You

How can my soul rest when it longs for its mate?
How can my mind sleep when obsessed
        with thoughts of you?
Through the darkness, I see your eyes watching me,
And hear gentle as an angel's breath
Words of love spoken through your lips
Sending notes of sacred music to my soul
Each a flower along the path to you.

Reply

We will walk through seasons unending
Unmarred by frozen nights and broiling suns
And find our place among the stars.

Path to You

Photo by **Frank Hajcak**

Healing Pool

Your heart – a pool of love
With the healing power of a thousand stars
Unlocking doors that hide wounds I bore,
Pain no one could see.

Monuments to old hurts crumble
Making my heart eager for love.

Reply

The fire that lights the stars
Ignites my heart
Consuming boundaries
Of day and night, life and death, you and I
Purifying our souls to seek love's destiny.

Passage to Love   _Photo by_ **_Frank Hajcak_**

Champion of Your Heart

Kiss me only if love fills
Every chamber of your heart
For when our lips touch I shall become your knight
And battle unto death whatever may hinder love's bond.

As your champion
I shall guard your soul with equal valor
So that your love and grace may grow
'Till angels bow in awe of your glory.

Reply

Inflamed with love
I offer my heart to you
My champion
Guard it with vigor and grace
As I shall guard yours.

Reply to Reply

Lady of love and grace
I swear upon the altar of all that is holy
To be your champion
As you shall be mine
May heaven so bind our souls.

Champion of Your Heart   _Photo by_ **_Frank Hajcak_**

First Kiss

As our lips touched in shyness
Three score and twice more
Cupids volley struck my heart
Igniting a pyrotechnic masterpiece
As the God of love applauded.

Reply

The rapture of loves' first kiss
Flowed through us like a river of dreams in endless nights
As heaven rejoiced and wedded our souls.

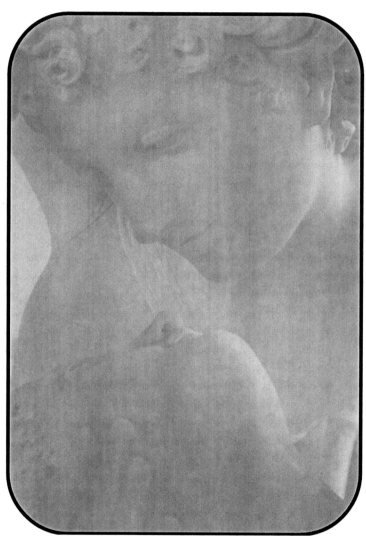

Love's First Kiss   *Photo by* **Frank Hajcak**

Reality?

I think of you
I speak of you
I dream of you
But where is reality?

Reply

I love you
You love me
Beyond that there is no reality.

(P.S. Where love is reality is not.
Does it really matter?)

Searching for Reality-Dali Mus. Spain   *Photo by **Frank Hajcak***

My Special Lady

What can I say to so wondrous a lady:
Who can stand on the moon and sing to the sea
And breathe through the universe her song of love
Who can capture the sun and let it shine from within
Who can fly to the stars and take their place
And light up the night with her smile of joy.

Reply

You heard my song
And felt my joy
Now share my love.

Empty Word

Love was an empty word
Hanging in the coldness of space.
You entered my life like a star gone nova
Embracing my heart with the heat of the sun.

Reply

Like melting snow in spring
Your words feed the roots of my love
Forcing my lips to seek your face
With flower-sweet kisses.
Locked like earth and moon
Our hearts play out their destiny.

Lullaby

Lady love I send to the heart
That beats within thy breast
One-Thousand kisses, each a lullaby
To sing thee to thy sleep
Perchance to dream of me.

Reply

With each kiss my heart melts
Like wax beneath the candle's flame
'Til embraced by slumber
With love filled dreams of you.

Detail of Painting by **Toulouse Lautrec**   **Musee d'Orsay,Paris**

Dreams of Eden

Lying in the garden
Legs and arms interlaced in love
Midday suns and midnight moons
Roll across the sky
Shaping dreams of Eden.

Reply

Wandering in dreams of Eden
Our hearts ascend to heavenly gardens.
Stars blooming in the grass
Moons birthing in ponds
Reflecting endless love.

Through Your Eyes

Awake daughter of love
Your man is at hand.
Through his eyes
You shall see your soul
And know that he loves you.
Through him you shall love yourself
And love with endless feeling
For your own soul is the fountain of strength,
Wisdom of life
And beauty of nature.

He shall drink of your fountain
Which will give him birth
To a new wholeness.
Through your eyes he shall see his soul
And know that you love him.
Through you he shall love himself
And you shall walk and play together
In a naked and shameless love,
Such is the beauty of nature.

Reply

The morning dawns
I take you in my arms
And gaze into your eyes.
Deep within I see myself
And feel your love
      Surrounding
      Caressing
      Strengthening.
Through you I love myself
And enter a new reality
Loving more deeply- more freely.
My soul overflows with wisdom and understanding
Treasuring life for we are of nature.

Soul Mate Kiss

Lost in enchantment between eyes and lips,
Our heads filled with the sweet wine
Of Love that cannot be undone
Lays bare the empire of the soul.

Reply

Love guides the heart
To the empire of the soul.
Your words reveal the pathway.

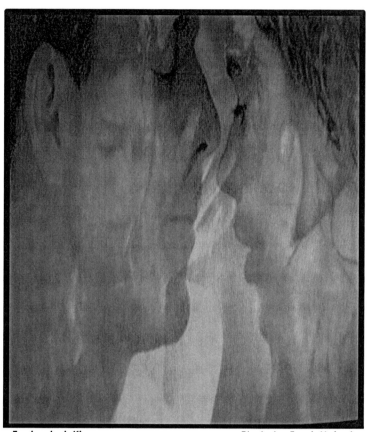

Enchanted Kiss *Photo by* **Frank Hajcak**

The Silent Song of Love

The soft flutter of butterfly wings
The delicate flight of the dandelion seed
The morning glory opening to greet the sun
Resplendent lilacs swaying in the warm spring breeze
My voice joins each silent note in praise of you.

Reply

I sense your voice in the silent
Ebb and flow of life around me.
My heart rejoices in each note
And bids me join the chorus
In gratitude for you.

Silent Love Songs   *Photos by **Frank Hajcak***

A Higher Plane

With heightened senses
I feel you touch my soul with love
That speaks with the heat of the sun
Awakening my heart to a higher plane of joy
Known only in dreams.

Reply

The love that bears no fruit but to love more
Binds our souls like molecules of a crystalline dream,
A gift beyond all blessings.

Crystalline Dream   *Photo by **Frank Hajcak***

Without You

My mind lost in a waking dream
Struggles to find its thoughts.
Helpless, like a bird clipped of its wings
My voice cannot find its tongue.
Without you
I am an empty gift box on Christmas morn.

Reply

Your words are precious glass seeds
Sown in my heart
Where they shall grow into diamonds
With infinite facets
Reflecting the love you brought into my life.

Glass Seeds   *Photo by* ***Frank Hajcak***

Corner of Creation

You stand so perfectly
In a special corner of creation
Ankle deep in stars
As if the Deity said
"Let there be grace and beauty and love."
What gift can I offer
In gratitude for you?

Reply

Like music from a star at the dawn of creation
Love reigns in heaven
And led me to your soul.
What thanks can we give but to love even more?

Starlight

You stand dreamlike
Bathed in starlight
My name rolls from your lips
Particles of golden dust
Seeding my heart with desire.

Reply

My heart sings your name
As I lay my love before you
In simple tenderness
Inviting a sacramental bond.

Invitation

You came into my life
With the promise of unending possibilities,
Your smile lingered in your eyes
Long after it left your lips
Inviting me to see into your soul
Hinting that love can be eternal.

Reply

Love surrounded us like a cathedral
Blessing our pilgrimage
To the altar where love begets love
Shattering the boundaries between heaven and earth.

Cathedral of Light
Photo by **Frank Hajcak**

Exchanging Vows

Exchanging vows
Our eyes met
Locking on pieces of dreams
Inflaming the heart with a bittersweet longing
That reveals the pathway to the soul.
You flow through me like a crystalline river
Preparing my heart for love.

Reply

The gifts you brought into my life
The light of joy
Warmth of love
And peace of soul.
What can I offer in return?

Reply to Reply

The gifts we give are the gifts we receive,
Receive from me the kiss that binds the soul.

Eruption

The silent air erupts with sweet notes of love
Full of grace and Godlike glory
Awakening my soul with images of you.
My name passes through your lips
With an intimacy that coaxes my heart
To follow but one rule
To love you more.

Reply

Breathing secrets of love you entered my soul
Each word a spark with the heat of the sun.
Like meteorites we streak across the sky
To the kingdom of love.

Dance of Love

Mesmerized by petal soft kisses
Lips moist with love's wine
Waiting to explore the sacred mysteries of love.
Like an apparition from beyond the stars
Our presence fills the sky
Parting the darkness with the rapture of a thousand suns.

Reply

In love shall we cling
Like petals to the flower,
'Til fish no longer swim
And the moon is dust in the solar winds.

Gravity

Moon tides pull us together,
Light and shadow wrapped in mystic silence.
As if by heavenly command
We dance in a symphony of starlight
Silent notes streaming through our souls.
We are reborn a star melting the limits of time.

Reply

Like the earth pulls the moon
And the sun the planets
In an endless dance
Our hearts seek their destiny
Drawn into an orbit of endless love.

Crowned With Love

Standing before me like a kingly apparition
You asked what will I give.
I searched my heart groping through
Shattered dreams and broken promises
Finding a mere spark of hope.
Weeping, offering my gift
You carried me to the sun
And crowned me with your love.

Reply

The sun is paled by the rising tide of love
Ignited by your words.
Like firebirds we streak across the sky
Singing
    One heart can burn with love
    Two hearts can outshine the sun.

Fresco-Church in Spain   Photo by **_Frank Hajcak_**

Sacramental Bond

You play my heart like a Stradivarius.
Sweet notes filling my soul
Choreographing a dance of joy,
A living prayer
Celebrating our sacramental bond.

Reply

Sweet notes flow from your heart
Silencing hurts and fears
Reshaping the boundaries of love
Imprinting in my heart the pathway to your soul.

Musical Prayer

Photo by **Frank Hajcak**

Daybreak

Dawn,
Riding the wings of a receding dream
Carrying ghost shadows from worlds
The waking eye cannot see
Giving rise to doubt.
Am I living in a love filled dream
Broken into endless fragments
Reflecting facets of you?
When dawn intrudes
Will your breath caress my cheek
Or will the light reveal you are only a dream?

Reply

The sun rose like a king
Bearing love of angelic purity
In a chalice of light
Sending angel soft kisses across our skin
Summoning love to flow into each other's cup
Lighting the way to our home in the stars.

Ghost Shadows   Photo by **Frank Hajcak**

Denial

The heart is denied by those who say:
    The lark does not sing in praise of love,
    The Rose does not bloom to express love,
    The moon does not shine to inspire love's bond,
    The soul does not exist to preserve love
        beyond the grave.
Since you entered my life my heart is no longer denied.

Reply

As if from the spell of love's dream
Angels whisper our names
Amidst the gentle cooing of mourning doves
Opening the door to eternal love.

Mourning Doves   Photo by **Frank Hajcak**

Divine Love

Prophets spoke of love
Born of heaven's womb:
Stars fueled by love
Leaping through the night
Like twin constellations
Touched by the hand of God.

Personified in your soul
Heaven bless that I may deserve
The golden glow of starlight
Held in your heart.

Reply

We must follow
Our hearts
For heaven's hand shall
Guide us from star to star
Bathing our souls with love
That knows no *Amen*.

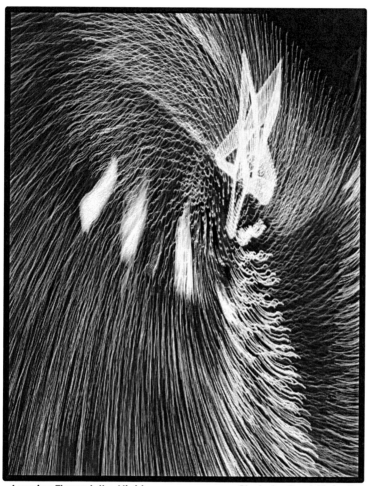

Leaping Through the Night   *Photo by* **Frank Hajcak**

The Angelus

I pray for love's song to enfold my heart
      in slumber sweet
Its words to cross my lips in praise of you.
To awaken at dawn with gratitude
For another day to love you.
At the noon hour I shall cast away all
 Save thoughts of you
And meditate on love's sweet ecstasy.
At evening tide, beneath a canopy of stars
Heaven's breath shall bind our souls.

Reply

I pray in slumber's sweet embrace
I hear your lips sing love's song
And awake at dawn with a heart
Inflamed with love for you.
And the noon hour finds
The fire stronger still
'Til at evening tide
Our souls bind in love's sweet ecstasy.

Detail of Millet's L'Angelus   *Musee d'Orsay Paris*

Love Me

Love me in the dance of joy
And in the darkest night
With all your heart.
Above all-
Love me in the silence of your soul for all eternity.

Reply

In the deep, golden silence of my soul
            where love begins
Your words twine 'round my heart
Like vines around the tree.
As I pledge unending love to you.

Dance of Joy   Photo by **Frank Hajcak**

The River

The whispering current carries angel voices
Singing ballads of soul mates
Walking in dewy meadows and verdant forests
Where golden suns and slivery moons
Dance across the sky
Weaving pathways like comet trails
Leading beyond the stars
Where time ends but love does not.

Reply

Within my heart lies a place
Where thoughts of you
Fill me with a joy
That knows no name.
I offer my heart to you
With the Oath to love you
As I do this day forevermore.

River in Yosemite   *Photo by **Frank Hajcak***

Friends and Lovers

You are the only person with whom
I have shared myself completely
You give me more than I ever ask
You are my friend and lover
I walk proudly and joyously beside you
I want to share my life with you.

Reply

Hand in hand we will walk
As friends and lovers
Laying bare our souls
New dreams to follow
New love to harvest.

Evening Prayer

May we never yield to sleep
With unshared love in our hearts
Or an un-given kiss on our lips.
May our last thoughts be of one another
And the joys we shared.
In slumber's sweet embrace
May our hearts dance in love filled dreams.

Reply

With all my heart and soul
I join in your prayer
And if this be slumber's dream
May I never wake.

Winds of Love

Alone like black mountains against an empty sky
My heart, echoes pleading coyote notes.
You rose as the moon
Your crystalline light surrounding, caressing the peaks
Filling me with songs of ancient soul mates from distant stars
Carried by the cosmic winds.

Reply

Galactic winds of love
Silencing songs of sorrows past
Nursing imperfections,
As buds about to bloom
Prepare our souls for celestial flight.

Moon Rise   Photo by **Trish Garwood**

My Prayer

I found prayer in the touch of your lips
Arms embracing me in soul mate love
With passion melting into dreams
Enfolded in a blanket of stars.

Reply

Your words
Like a sea of flowers
Harvesting the sweetness of the sun
Shape the prayer that binds our souls.

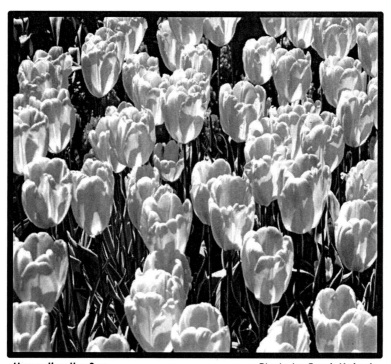

Harvesting the Sun   *Photo by* **Frank Hajcak**

Queen of the Stars

The grace of God
Filled your heart
Touched your soul
And raised you beyond the noblest of queens
To your special place among the stars.
I pray heaven will meld my soul
Into the band of gold that holds your heart
The diamond that outshines the sun.

Reply

You touch my heart with love
That knows no bounds
Awakening my soul to a higher plane.

Ineffable love

I think of you, speak of you, dream of you
My eyes are blind to all but you.
Gentle fires race across my skin,
Each moment giving rise to yet another tender ache.

In search of relief I chase you from my mind
But the thoughts return a hundred fold,
Forcing your name across my lips
Commanding my heart to open the gates of love.
Still, no words find my tongue.

Reply

Words are but obstacles that stem the flow of love.
The heart knows what the tongue cannot speak
And fills the silence between words with love.
May our words be few.

Ode to Our Love

May the sun of long life shine upon you,
My love surround you
And the light of joy guide you
Through the darkness that may befall you.
May you find the beauty I see within you
Before your soul decides to leave you.

May choirs of angels be there to greet you
With the love I failed to give you
The peace that overlooked you
And the joy that passed by you
When your soul decides to leave you.

Reply

May the sun of long life shine upon us,
The love we share surround us
And the light of joy guide us
Through the darkness that may befall us.
May we share the beauty within us
Before our souls decide to leave us.

Angelic Greeting   *Photo by **Frank Hajcak***

Transformation

As the rising sun transforms the earth
From grey shadow to vivid color
Your love transforms my life.
Notes become symphonies
        Words-poems
        Threads-tapestries.

Life became art.

Reply

Your love revealed secrets
        Unlocked my heart
        Released my soul.
Everything I see, hear, touch and feel
        Is so much more.
We are the symphony
        The poem
        The tapestry.

Love became Art.

How do I Love Thee?

How do I love thee?
Let me count the ways.
As eagerly as the honey bee
Enters the first flower of spring
And the morning glory greets the dawn.
As gently as the sun kisses away the morning dew
And the moon reflects the sun.
As completely as the sky enfolds the earth
And night surrounds the stars.
As passionately as the virgin's first love
With a depth and breadth
Expanding each moment beyond measure.
Thus shall I love thee
Till the breath of life no longer flows.
Then joined by choirs of angels
I shall love thee even more.

Reply

My heart, quivering with love can find no words
To greet thy pledge.
I shall bask in the joy of a love so gentle
Eager, passionate and complete
'til my soul is overfilled
and repay thee each day a-hundred fold
'til life no longer flows.
Then joined by myriads of angels
We shall love forevermore.

Returning

Events cannot tarnish
Time cannot weaken
The love we create,
Heart bound to heart
Soul to soul
Backed by the ancient pool of love
To which we all must return,
Adding our offering
So others may easier find their way
Through the darkness between the stars.

Reply

Our lives form a story of closeness and grace
Blessed beyond dreams
Flowing through galaxies
Carrying the ancient code of love
That began and ends at heaven's door.

Machu Picchu   *Photo by* **Frank Hajcak**

So This is Love

So this is love
The kind that's beyond dreams and fantasy
That makes you dance and sing like Cinderella.
So this is love
The kind you're afraid to wish for more
Because you might implode into tiny bits of star dust
And end up in another galaxy
Where the only thing you know
 Is the voice inside your head
Singing of love that sends seismic shivers
    through your soul
Casting spells that make stars collide
Creating black hole gravity
From which there is no desire to escape.
So this is love
The kind you brought into my life.

Voice in My Head   *Photo by* **Frank Hajcak**

Reply

Yes this is love,
The kind that makes you feel like you're standing
    on the edge of the universe
Drinking in the light of a trillion suns
Savoring the moment love was born,
Living that moment – every moment
    Sharing it with soul deep understanding
    Sheltered by Heaven's door.
Yes this is love,
The kind you brought into my life.

Light of a Trillion Suns   Photo by **Frank Hajcak**

Your Personal Invitation

Dear Reader,

Midnight Harvest: Living in the Moment of Love is our song that led to soulmate love. We believe that every heart has its own love song and that every couple can discover their own path to soulmate love.

You are cordially invited to visit us at www.FrankHajcak.com. There you will find a variety of tools, ideas and guidelines for composing your own song of love.

Warm Regards,
Frank & Tricia

Special Thanks To ...

George *and* **Norma Garwood** and **Dean** *and* **Elaine Holbrook** for being outstanding examples of deep and loving relationships that have always been a source of inspiration and hope.

Joy Shelton for her encouragement, many suggestions, hours of her time and contributions for the companion relationship enrichment manual (see page 94).

Hinda-Jonathan *and* **the Orlando Poetry Troupe** for giving us our first opportunity to read selections from *Midnight Harvest: Living in the Moment of Love* publicly in Orlando.

Donna *and* **Bernie Case** for their evaluation and encouragement to share our work with others.

Finally, to my son **Greg** who taught me the importance of word economy in poetry.

About the Authors

Frank Hajcak, Ph.D. and Tricia Garwood, MS maintained a joint private practice and consulting firm specializing in self-empowerment and relationship enrichment in the Philadelphia area for over 25 years. Their first book, on sustaining long term relationships, was the main selection of the **Psychology Today**, the **Psychiatric and Social Science** and the **Behavioral Science** book clubs, translated into French, Polish and Estonian and featured in Glamour magazine.

Tricia and Frank discovered that poetry is a powerful tool for relationship enrichment. The authors stated, "Poetry bypasses the logical defenses of the rational mind and links directly to the heart. In a few words a poetic image can catapult a couple into the depth and intensity of soul mate love in a way that would take many pages of prose or days of discourse. Couples quickly appreciate the value of *Midnight Harvest: Living in the Moment of Love* as an immediate source of enrichment and personal growth."

The authors have lectured and given workshops throughout North America. Both are also noted for their work and publications in art and photography. They reside in Florida where they offer workshops and classes in creativity and writing poetry for relationship enrichment.

Other Books by the Authors

Hidden Bedroom Partners debunks Freudian myths and offers an alternate perspective on inhibited sexual desire, sexual addiction and why we do what we do in the bedroom. Main selection of the **Psychology Today**, the **Psychiatric and Social Science** and the **Behavioral Science** book clubs. Translated into French, Polish and Estonian. Featured and quoted in **Glamour, Cosmopolitan,** Journal of Family Therapy, Journal of Adolescence and Ann Landers advice column.

Expanding Creative Imagination introduces **Active Perception** as the key to personal creative development that will give you and your children the creative edge. The authors gave **Active Perception** the ultimate test. They applied it to various avocations and succeeded in becoming published children's authors and illustrators, photographers, artists, cartoonists, musicians and poets. Quoted in *Gifted Child Quarterly, Disney's Family Fun, Scholastic Arts, Lens, Petersen's Photographic* and *Photo Life.* Originally published in 1993. Korean edition 1995. Still a classic.

Rising Sun, a picture book for children and families, is an environmental fable about a Native American youth sent on a mission to learn the secrets of nature and become the wise leader of his people. Endorsed by **Chief Halftown** of the Seneca Nation, **Earth Justice, The Lakota Deer Chasers** and chosen twice as the book of the year by the Mayor of Philadelphia **for Pennsylvania's** *Books Not Guns* anti-violence reading program.

Great Moments in Olympic History is the only cartoon book in the world on the Olympics. Endorsed by former PHILADELPHIA EAGLE, FRANK LEMASTER, *Great Moments* is essentially **three books in one**:
   B.C. Games: How Neanderthals competed and developed some   basic rules.
   Modern Games: What you won't see on TV.
   Future Games 3000 AD - The Supreme Being sweeps the gold as genetically perfected super athletes learn the real fun is not winning but how you play the game.

Forthcoming Books

Secrets of Soulmate Love: The eight laws of love culled from cognitive behavioral psychology plus many more secrets all proven to set you on the path to soulmate love.

Midnight Harvest Relationship Enrichment Manual: Activities and exercises based on verses from *Midnight Harvest: Living in the Moment of Love*, that will keep you on the path to soulmate love.

Wisdom to Live By: Original, short thought provoking insights that will help you overcome obstacles, find personal fulfillment and achieve your best life. For example:

Fear is courage waiting to happen.

The eye can only see what the mind is willing to accept.